Challenge Your Child

KEVIN SMITH

ISBN: 9798764722580

Table of Contents

Acknowledgements

This book would not have been possible without the thoughts and guidance of experienced educators.

To begin, I truly thank my wife Cathy and friend John Sturtevant for their years of teaching and service to students. Their constant support, insights and suggestions contributed greatly to this text.

I would also like to thank Dr. Jane Vella who is considered to be a world renowned expert in Teaching through Dialogue. Jane is the founder of Global Learning Partners (www. globallearningpartners.com). GLP continues to offer the rich principles and practices of a learning-centered approach called "Dialogue Education". I first read Jane's book "Training through Dialogue" over 25 years ago. Her thoughts and concepts have shaped every class or meeting I have had the responsibility to lead. Jane's willingness to review my writing, give feedback and gracious support has helped immensely.

I also thank Dr. Michael Kessler. Michael is a physician with his own training organization. Michael gives a detailed overview of how physicians are trained and how it often differs from the way most students are taught. Some of the concepts I have learned from Michael have shaped my thoughts on education and how the Challenging process can be used in a modified version by parents on a regular basis. I will share some of these thoughts particularly when discussing how parents can challenge their older students.

Preface

I am a former teacher. I've worked with school-aged children for about 10 years. I have children of my own, and now I have grandchildren. Over the course of my career as a parent and a teacher, I found myself continuously surprised by the observant and inquisitive nature of children. However, it is not necessarily intuitive for adults to engage children in a way that guides them towards deeper thinking and understanding.

I know how difficult it can be for many parents to find ways and time to participate in their child's education. I also know helping with homework can be frustrating at times. I wrote *Challenge Your Child* for busy parents who want tips and tools for supporting their child's educational growth.

I understand that parents might not have the time to read a long instruction manual, so I've made this book intentionally short, the sort of book you can read in an evening. I also designed it to be a reference, with easy-to-find sections that you can refer back to refresh your memory as your child grows up.

I offer tips and examples for engaging with your child starting prior to pre-school age, all the way through young adulthood. The concepts are simple. The examples I offer can get you going right away, without any preparation.

I hope you find *Challenge Your Child* to be useful, engaging, and fun!

Kevin

Introduction

Challenge Your Child is a powerful teaching technique designed to help parents and caregivers take an active role in their child's education. Naturally, most parents want to help their children learn and achieve as much as possible. While they have the desire and see the need, they also think:

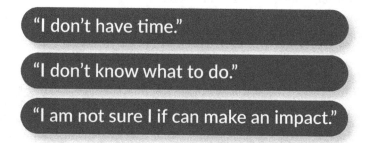

"I don't have time."

"I don't know what to do."

"I am not sure I if can make an impact."

My hope is that after reading *Challenge Your Child,* you will be convinced that you can make a difference. In this book, you will learn a simple process to help you instantly assess what your child knows, as well as what they need to learn. You will also learn how you can use this process anywhere, taking advantage of the many opportunities that come up daily to create educational dialogue. You can challenge your child while in the car, during meals, while helping out with homework, or any other time you're together with your child. If you travel or are separated from your child for periods of time, *Challenge Your Child* can help you play an active role in your child's education using your cell phone or computer as you communicate online. And you can use this program with children of any age and learning capability.

The essence of the *Challenge Your Child* concept is daily educational dialogue between parents and children using questions and repetition to, very literally, challenge your child. In the following pages, I will introduce you to the question types that are at the heart of this program (open ended questions and follow-up questions) and how to use these questions to challenge your child to think, problem solve, and verbalize. My intention is that as you engage in this very simple dialogue process with your child, you learn how to create a positive, supportive learning environment, and most importantly, that you nurture or help your child to develop an "I Can" attitude for learning and academic challenges. Using this program every day, you can contribute significantly to your child's education and confidence for many years to come.

This program is simple, so keep it simple. Start off by setting a simple goal: engage in a question and answer session with your child at least once *every day,* and build up from there to perhaps a couple of interactions per day. You can have these educational interactions in a wide variety of situations, as I mentioned earlier: in the car, at dinner, before bed, and especially during structured homework time. (It will result in you making greater contributions to your child's educational experience and enjoying your shared learning time!)

By way of example, here are a few topic areas that lend themselves to the *Challenge Your Child* method:

Younger children:
Numbers, letters, colors, shapes, animals, simple math problems

Older children:
Spelling, math, science, history, geography, literature, current events, life events, religion, if appropriate.

You might be surprised how many children love these challenge opportunities.

Some days you might not have the time for an educational interaction with your child or it might have to take place quickly. If you miss a day, no problem. Start up again the next day. Just don't give up! This is not a program where you need to block 30-60 minutes of time every day; this is a program that fits today's lifestyle. You can use it anytime, anywhere.

Objectives:

By the time you complete this booklet, you will be able to:

1. Create educational dialogue with children of any age and learning capability, anytime, anywhere.

2. Understand the question types that are the drivers of *Challenge Your Child* and how to use them to create educational dialogue.

3. Use these question types and repetition to challenge your child to think, problem solve, and verbalize.

4. Create a positive, supportive learning environment.

5. Work towards turning "I can't do it" into "I can."

6. Accomplish all these goals with minimal planning time, materials and expense: just you, your child, materials on hand, and dialogue!

What You Can Expect with Regular Use of the *Challenge Your Child* format?

As with all things, use this process in moderation but routinely. If you do, you will experience the following:

- An increase in educational dialogue with your child.

- A greater sense of what your child knows and needs to learn.

- Your child will know more, in greater depth and as such, be much more confident in learning situations.

- You will challenge your child to think, problem solve, and verbalize. Can you think of more important skills? As you ask an open ended question, watch your child's face as they work to come up with and explain an answer. Once you understand that you have the power to challenge, you will understand why so many teachers love their jobs. The ultimate high for a teacher is knowing they have helped a child learn. It feels even better for a parent. *Challenge Your Child* will help you create these learning experiences.

- You will create many repetition opportunities. Repetition is a great teacher. Using the *Challenge Your Child* format is a great way to build the repetition opportunities needed to help your child increase knowledge and broaden their understanding of any topic you choose.

- When asking challenge questions, your child will sometimes give good or correct answers. This creates opportunities for praise or pats on the back. Your child's confidence will grow. So much of a child's success in school comes from confidence. Confidence is created by success through repetition. You will be creating these success opportunities.

- When asking challenge questions, you will sometimes get wrong answers or "I don't knows." These responses will reveal to you the learning your child needs. You have now created a teaching opportunity. You can explain, discuss and challenge again, repeatedly if necessary, to make sure your child understands.

As knowledge grows and confidence increases through dialogue, repetition, and positive support, your child will come to enjoy the educational challenges that come from you and in school. In some cases, "I can't do it" will become "I can." For other children, those who thrive on academic challenges, the joy of being challenged will simply add to their thirst and competitive drive to learn more.

Now, let's dive in!

This Teaching technique utilizes a question and answer format. We will discuss three types of questions and it's very important to understand the differences. They are:

 Close ended questions
(usually get a yes or a no, or a one-word answer)

 Open ended questions
(cannot be answered with a yes or a no)

 Follow up questions
(also open ended, asked after your child answers a previous opened ended question)

While you need to know about close ended questions, the major focus of this program is on open ended and follow up questions. Follow up questions and repetition are the key to taking knowledge and learning to a higher level.

Close Ended Questions

Generally speaking, close ended questions are answered with a yes or no or a one-word answer. Little to no dialogue comes from close ended questions unless the child chooses to elaborate.

Close ended questions are necessary at times and will get you direct answers. Use this question type when needed, but for this program, focus primarily on the other types of questions. In most cases you can create open ended questions that will initiate better dialogue and get more information than you can achieve with close ended questions.

Examples of close ended questions:

Did you do your math homework? This is a close ended question requiring a yes or no answer.

Are you ready for your spelling test on Friday? Again, a yes or no question.

Let's say you pull a crayon out of a box. If you ask, *"Is this color green?"* you have asked a direct yes or no question. Your child's answer will tell you if they know the color, but little else. Your child might also be guessing. As you will see, open ended questions will offer better challenge and discussion opportunities.

Close ended questions are sometimes necessary, but you will want to focus on open ended questions. Open ended questions will challenge your child to a much greater degree, and you will gain a lot more information about what your child knows and needs to learn.

Open Ended Questions

Open ended questions usually begin with

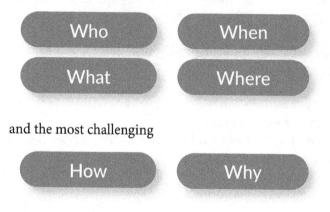

Who

When

What

Where

and the most challenging

How

Why

Questions starting with these words cannot be answered with a yes or no.

Answers to open ended questions can be anything from "I don't know" or a shoulder shrug to the most confident and in-depth answers imaginable.

Whenever possible, ask open ended questions. Typically, more in-depth answers will come from open ended questions. This question type is great at assessing what your child knows and needs to learn. Thinking, problem-solving, and verbalization can be challenged to a greater degree with open ended questions. Open ended questions start a dialogue.

Let's review two of the close ended questions mentioned previously and see how they can be re-formulated as open ended questions:

Close ended:
Did you do your math homework?

Open ended:
What was the most challenging math problem in your homework tonight?

This open ended question has challenged your child to think and verbalize. Your child has to think back to the homework, pick the toughest problem, and begin to explain or show you what the issue or challenge is. You are now in a dialogue! You will be able to assess exactly what your child is learning, how well they understand the topic, and what help they need for improvement.

Close ended:
Are you ready for your spelling test on Friday?

Open ended:
What are the 2 most challenging words from your spelling list this week?

Again, your child will be challenged to think and verbalize, and encouraged to share key information. With their answer to your open ended question, you will learn the biggest challenges from your child's perspective, and this can initiate discussion to help improve their understanding.

Other Examples of Open Ended Questions

 Let's say you just finished reading a book to your pre-school child at bedtime:

> In your own words, **what** was the story about?
>
> **What** did you like most about the story?
>
> **Who** was your favorite character (person) in the story?
>
> **What** character in the story reminds you most of yourself? **Why**?
>
> **What** was the happiest (saddest) part of the story?

 Let's say you are talking to a primary grade-level child and you have a handful of change equaling 72 cents:

> **How** much money do I have here?
>
> **What** is the coin here with the most value?
>
> **What** is the coin here with the least value?
>
> **What** would you rather have, 3 nickels or one quarter? **Why**?
>
> **How** much more would I need to make one dollar?
>
> **What** are some of the things you can do to earn money?

I hope you are starting to see how your child's thinking, problem solving, and verbalization skills are challenged through this type of dialogue. You can probably also begin to see how one good open ended question naturally leads to follow up question possibilities.

Follow Up Questions

Simply put, follow up questions are also open ended questions. Listen to your child's answer to the first question and craft another open ended question to expand the challenge or learning opportunity.

Open ended questions check for understanding and begin the process of challenging your child to think, problem solve, and verbalize. Follow-up questions allow you to further challenge your child's knowledge, understanding or ability to figure out an answer. Follow up questions will add depth to your discussions. Follow up questions will add to your child's knowledge base.

Think about this for a second: **YOU** have the opportunity and ability to add to your child's knowledge and depth of understanding for any topic you choose. **Consistent use of follow up questions will be a major factor in your success with using** *Challenge Your Child.*

Examples of Follow Up Questions:

Keeping with the money theme to make it simple, let's say you have a handful of change equaling 67 cents. In talking with your primary grade-level student, you ask:

Open ended question:
How much money do I have here?

Follow up possibilities:
If I take away a nickel from 67 cents, **how** much do I have now?

If I add a dime to the 67 cents, **how** much do I have now?

If I have 67 cents and buy candy for 50 cents, **how** much money will I have left?

I have 67 cents now. **How** much more money would I need to equal one dollar?

Why do people put their money in banks?

Besides putting money in the bank, **what** else can people do to save or invest?

Dwell on this example for a moment:

An interaction with just one open ended question and one follow up question can create a Challenge and Learning opportunity that take just a matter of seconds. Your open ended question gives you the opportunity to assess what your child knows or needs to learn. The follow up allows you to further challenge and assess what your child knows or can figure out.

If you were to ask your child all seven questions listed in the example, this learning opportunity would take just a matter of moments, while key math skills would be challenged and important discussion about money management could occur.

You can accomplish a lot of learning in a short period of time if you choose.

Another example:
Looking at a map of the United States with your 4th grader:

Open ended question:
Where on the map is our home state?

Follow up possibilities:
What state is directly north of our state?

What state is directly south?

What large body of water is closest to our state?

If we want to drive to New York state, **what** states would we drive through?

What state would you like to visit most? **Why**?

Why do we have states?

One more example for parents who frequently travel for work. During your call home, ask your child to pull out a map or pull one up online to share. Remind your child what city you are in. You might ask the following:

Open ended question:
What state am I in?

Possible follow ups:
What states did I drive through (or fly over) to get here?

What can you tell me about this state?

What states border the state I am in?

How would living in this state be different than our home state?

You could go on forever! The bottom line: no matter the age, even with children as young as 2 and 3 years old, you can start to challenge with age-appropriate questions and have some amazing educational interactions.

Examples By Age Group

Let's look at examples of open ended and follow up questions for children and students of different ages that can be used to create challenge opportunities.

You can begin using *Challenge Your Child* with children as young as 2 to 3 years old or a year to 18 months prior to preschool. You might be surprised how much children this age can learn with consistent challenges, dialogue and repetition. Here are very simple examples in a variety of day to day situations:

 While walking down the street:

Open ended:
What numbers do you see on that house?

Follow up:
Why do houses have numbers?

Open ended:
What letters do you see on the stop sign?

Follow up:
Why do we have Stop signs?

Open ended:
What color is this car?

Follow up:
How many blue cars do you see on our street?

At dinner:

How many forks are on the table?

How many forks plus spoons are on the table?

What shape is our table?

What shapes do you see our kitchen?

How high can you count today?

How high can you count by 2s? **How** high can you count by 5s?

Sitting at a Red light:

What color is the light now?

What do the colors on the traffic light mean?

At a Yield sign:

Open ended:
What shape is the yellow sign?

Follow ups:
What letters do you see on the sign?

What does yield mean?

What is the difference between a yield sign and a stop sign?

 At the Grocery store:

Open ended:
What colors do you see on this cereal box?

Follow ups:
What letters do you know on this box?

Where does this cereal come from?

Open ended question:
What numbers do you see telling the price for this gallon of milk?

Follow up:
How does the milk get from the cow to the store?

In these last two examples, your child might not know where the cereal comes from or how the milk gets from the cow to the store. These may end up being teaching opportunities where you have to explain. That said, you have just educated your child on the bigger picture and added to their knowledge and understanding, all while just doing your regular shopping.

 Reading one of your child's favorite books about animals:

Open ended:
What animal is this?

Follow ups:
What other animals do you see on this page?

What is the biggest (smallest) animal you see on this page?

How many animals do you see on this page?

How is the elephant different from the other animals you see here?

What animal(s) in this picture live on a farm? **What** animal(s) in this picture might live in a zoo?

What is one animal here we could never have as a pet? **Why?**

You can see the teaching and learning opportunities open ended questions like these begin to create. You can also envision any number of follow up questions you might create to take learning to another level.

Please remember the importance games can have in the learning process, even for very young children. Board games, card games, computer games, even sport stats can create powerful learning opportunities that can be enhanced by using the *Challenge Your Child* skills. Board games and card games usually require strategy which challenges thinking and problem-solving skills. These games create many repetition opportunities and also teach about taking turns, winning and losing, and other socialization skills.

Example: Cards
Let's say you have a deck of cards. You can create many challenge opportunities here.

> **Open ended:**
> Pull 5 cards from the deck and hand them to your child. **How** many cards do you have?
>
> Pull a different amount of cards and repeat to work on counting skills.
>
> **Follow ups:**
> Hold up different number cards such as a 7 of diamonds or a 5 of Hearts. Ask: **What** number is this? Repeat.
>
> Show two number cards. Ask: If we add the numbers on these two cards together, **how** much would it be? Repeat with different number combinations.
>
> **Follow ups continued:**
> Pick five number cards. Ask: **How** would you put these cards in numerical order from smallest to largest?
>
> Pick five different number cards. Ask: **How** would you put these cards in numerical order from largest to smallest?

Perhaps finish up by playing a card game appropriate for your child's age. Challenges and the number of repetitions card games or board games can provide young children will help to increase your child's understanding of number basics.

The goal here is to show some of the many learning opportunities in daily life for very young children. Your focus on letters, numbers, colors, and shapes, in addition to simple math problems and dialogue while reading will add to your child's knowledge and depth of knowledge for any topic or concept you choose.

A gentle reminder! While many examples are listed here, try to focus on just a couple of challenges each day. If you overdo it, it could become more like a task for your child and it might be tougher to get positive participation.

If your child is in school, take your cue from the work or materials coming home. Challenge Your Child will help you assess what your child knows and needs to learn. This program will also help you take learning and understanding to a much greater level. Additionally, we will look at opportunities outside of school where you can create challenges.

Examples while reviewing various materials coming home from school:

 Numbers:

Open ended:
Pointing to a number on a worksheet:

Ask: **What** number is this? (5)

Follow ups:
What number comes before/after this number?

If I add 2 to 5, **how** much will it be?

If I take 3 from 5, **how** much will it be?

If I have two 5s, **how** much is it? **How** about three 5s?

What number can you think of that is greater than (less then) 5?

When you think of the number 5, **what** coin comes to mind?

Letters:

Pointing to a letter on a homework page

Ask: **What** letter is this? (H)

Follow ups:
What names do you know that start with the letter H?

What items can you buy at the grocery store that begin with the letter H?

What other words do you know that begin with H?

What letter comes before (after) H in the alphabet?

What sound would the letter H make in the word help?

How would you create a sentence with two words that begin with H?

Colors:

Pointing to an assignment page focused on colors:

Ask: **Where** on this page do you see the color green?

What other colors do you see on this page?

What foods are green?

What animal(s) are green?

What can you think of outside that is green?

How do you spell green?

What letters in the word green are consonants? **What** letter(s) are vowels?

How many letters are there in the word green?

Shapes:

Open ended:

Pointing to a triangle from an online assignment:

Ask: **What** shape is this?

Follow ups:

How is a triangle different from a square?

How is a square different from a rectangle?

How many different shapes can you name and draw?

How many different shapes can you find in this room?

What items outside our house can you think of that have a square shape?

How would you use the word "triangle" in a sentence?

What letters in the word triangle are not consonants?

Examples outside of school:

 Reading your child's favorite book (you reading to your child, or perhaps your child reading to you).

Open ended:
What was the story about? (Thinking, comprehension, verbalizing)

Follow ups:
Who (or **What**) was your favorite character in the story? **Why?** (Thinking and verbalizing)

If you could change one thing about the story, **what** would it be? (Thinking, verbalization)

Pointing to a particular word: **What** word is this? **What** does this word mean? **How** would you use this word in a sentence? (Recognition, thinking, creativity, verbalization)

Do a quick math challenge before dinner. Write a number on a piece of paper and ask:

> Open ended:
> **What** number is this? (7)
>
>
> Follow ups:
> **What** number comes before 7?
>
> **What** number comes after 7?
>
> If I take 2 from 7, **how** much would I have?
>
> If I add 2 to 7, **how** much would I have?
>
> **How** much is 7 plus 7?

Math challenges can go on and on. You can do so many math problems in so little time. Opportunities are everywhere.

Dice
Let's say you have a couple of dice from a board game. You can use these to create several questions. Let's use three dice as an example:

Open ended:
How many dice do I have here?

Follow ups:
Point to a number on one of the dice. Ask: **What** number is this? Repeat.

Roll three dice. Ask:

If you add up the total here, **how** much would it be?

Roll the dice again. Ask:

How much do we have now?

Roll the dice again. Ask:

What dice here have a number greater than 2?

Roll the dice again. Ask:

What dice here have a number less than 5?

Other possible follow ups:
What is the highest possible amount you would have for all three dice?

What would be the lowest amount possible amount for all three dice?

Why are dice needed in many different games?

Example: Same Versus Different

Suppose you want to explore this concept with your child. Same versus different is a great way to challenge your child's analytical thinking and verbalization skills. Answers to the initial questions you ask are sometimes easy and obvious, but as you dig deeper, you will challenge your child's thinking and verbalization, and some interesting thoughts and answers can follow.

 Let's use a stop sign and a stop light as an example.

Open ended:
Looking at a stop sign and a stop light, in **what** two ways are they similar?

Follow ups:
In **what** two ways are they different?

What other similarities could there be?

What other differences could there be?

What would happen if there were no stop signs or stop lights?

What would happen if there were no stop lights, only stop signs?

Other possible Same Versus Different topics:

A car versus a bus

A soccer ball versus a basketball

Stairs versus an elevator

Seeing versus hearing

I am sure you can think of other examples as well. Similar versus different or compare and contrast will challenge your child to see connections and think about objects or ideas in unique ways. These questions will challenge your child's thinking and verbalization while also developing their understanding. This ability to analyze similarities and differences will serve your child well as they move forward in education and beyond.

Parents of pre-school and kindergarten-age children have a great opportunity to help their children to get off to a solid start with academics. The examples listed using *Challenge Your Child* are just a few of the opportunities available to you each day to take an active role in your child's education.

Primary Grades

You will have many opportunities to challenge your child with questions and repetition while they are in the primary grades. Again, take your cue from the schoolwork coming home. The challenges and repetition you create will go a long way in creating a strong academic foundation. Remember back to your youth when you used flash cards and multiplication tables? They were designed to create the repetition necessary to make sure you understood the material and that it became ingrained. Consistent repetition with Challenge Your Child will help to ensure what is being taught in school can in many cases become ingrained and second nature. Math, reading and language arts will be key subject areas. Science will also be part of the curriculum. Homework and textbooks will keep you on track.

Some examples and ideas to help you with repetition:
Buy, make—or have your child make—flashcards for math, spelling, phonics, etc. Use these teaching tools to challenge and create repetition.

Review the spelling list assigned each week. Challenge for spelling, definitions, sentence use, synonyms, and antonyms.

Create a variety of five to ten math problems aligned with the current schoolwork for a challenge.

Have your child read you a story, an article, or even just a paragraph from a book. Many challenge questions can be created from this material. (Later, I will say more on the importance of listening to your child read.)

Review homework assignments using *Challenge Your Child*. These challenges will help you assess how well your child knows the material. You will also be able to add to the depth of knowledge through your follow up questions. In some cases, your child may end up teaching you something you did not know.

Repetition is **SO** important in creating a true understanding of the material being taught. Teachers will do their best to create repetition opportunities, but in many cases it will not be enough. This is where *Challenge Your Child* and your efforts can help significantly.

If your child gains confidence through repetition and positive feedback, they will handle challenges in school as opportunities. Your child will enjoy solving problems and have the confidence to do so. If your child does not have confidence, the "I can't do it" comment and the frustration that goes with it will occur more frequently. This creates an uphill battle.

Examples Pertaining to School:

 Spelling

Let's say you are helping your child review the spelling list for the week. We will use the word drive as the example.

> **Open ended:**
> **How** do you spell the word drive?
>
> **Follow ups:**
> **What** does drive mean?
>
> **What** other possible meanings can you think of for the word drive?
>
> **How** would you use the word drive in a sentence as a noun?
>
> **How** would you use drive in a sentence as a verb?
>
> **What** words mean about the same thing as the word drive?
>
> **What** words rhyme with drive?

Language Arts
Let's say your child has a homework page focusing on nouns and verbs.

Open ended:

How would you explain the difference between a noun and a verb?

What three examples can you give me for nouns? (verbs)

Follow ups:
Looking at a page from one of your child's favorite books. Point to a sentence. Ask:

Where is the noun and the verb in this sentence? Repeat

How would you write a sentence using one of your spelling words as a noun?

How would you write a sentence using one of your spelling words as a verb?

What words can you think of that could be used as a noun in one situation and a verb in another?

Clocks/Time

Let's say your child is learning about telling time and you want to present a challenge to create extra repetitions to help in learning this concept.

Open ended:

It takes 30 minutes for you to get to school each day. If school starts at 8:00, **what** time will we need to leave?

Follow ups:

If it took 45 minutes to travel to school, **what** time would we need to leave?

Where on the clock would the hour and minute hands be for 7:30? 7:15?

What time is it now?

What time will it be in 90 minutes?

What does quarter after the hour mean?

What does half past the hour mean?

What is the difference between AM and PM?

+	−
×	=

Math Challenge

Let's say you and your child are waiting at a doctor's office for an appointment and you want to try a quick math challenge which closely aligns with the homework assignments coming home.

Open ended:
How much is 25 plus 14?

Follow ups:
If I add 13 to that amount, **how** much do I have?

So now we are at 52. **How** much would I have if I double that number?

How much do I have if I divide 52 in half?

What number plus 52 equals 100?

If I subtract 29 from 52, **how** much would I have?

If I divide 52 by 4, **what** would the answer be?

Why is it so important for you to know how to add and subtract?

What jobs require you to be good at math?

Again, with math, you can ask so many questions and go in many different directions in very little time. You can also do it anywhere. Repetition will help your child build a strong base in the skills and concepts being taught.

Examples Outside of School:

Let's look at a couple of examples outside of school where you can create challenges to reinforce concepts your child is learning in school.

Sporting Event
You are at a baseball game with your child. You decide to buy a soda and a hot dog for your child.

> Open ended:
> If the soda costs 3 dollars and the hot dog costs 4 dollars, **what** will the total cost be?
>
> Follow ups:
> If I give the cashier 10 dollars to pay for the cost of the hot dog and soda and told you, you can keep the change it you get the answer correct, **how** much change should you get back?
>
> If we buy 2 hot dogs and 2 soft drinks, **what** will the cost be?
>
> If I give the cashier 20 dollars to pay for the 2 hot dogs and 2 sodas, **how** much should I get back?
>
> **Why** is it so important to know how to count your change accurately?

Hibernation

Let's say it's autumn, and you see squirrels running around the yard. You can explore the idea of hibernation. You might watch an online video with your child to create a more in-depth learning opportunity and additional dialogue for this topic.

Open ended:

What type of food do squirrels gather?

Follow ups:

Why do squirrels gather so much food in the fall?

Where do squirrels put the food?

How do squirrels stay warm in the winter?

How would you explain hibernation to your teacher?

What surprised you the most as you watched this video about squirrels and hibernation?

One more critical example: Reading!!

Reading proficiency will be a major factor in your child's academic success. Having your child read out loud to you does two things. First, it consistently creates the repetition needed for your child's development. Secondly, it gives you the opportunity to assess changes in their skill level and progress with pronunciations, and confidence, as just a few examples. Vary the reading between favorite books, stories, homework, articles, or something online. Use *Challenge Your Child* to check for comprehension and to create additional learning opportunities.

Reading repetition is so important for many reasons; reading skill is the basis for learning. It will also be part of every standardized test your child will take. In addition, reading out loud begins to develop the public speaking skills that will be very important as your child moves forward in school and beyond. Children who have strong oral reading skills are often picked for leadership opportunities that arise in school. Repetition with reading out loud will be time well spent.

To summarize, the use of open ended questions, follow up questions, and repetition during the primary grades will help to make sure important learning concepts become ingrained and second nature. Challenging will help ensure your child can use this knowledge in a wide variety of ways and circumstances. The challenges you create today may be similar to the challenges your child's teacher will be using soon.

If you become aware that your child is having trouble with any particular issue, bring it up to your child's teacher for discussion and help. Being proactive when concerns arise will start the process of getting your child the help they need.

Again, follow the homework trail. At this point, I think you understand how you can use open ended and follow up questions along with repetition to make sure key learning materials are fully understood.

That said, some of the material your child is learning may be a challenge for you. Using Challenge Your Child, you do not need to be an expert in all cases. If your child is really on top of things, you don't need to know the answers necessarily; you just need the right questions to challenge your child to explain and teach you. This is a powerful teaching concept. Teachers often use this technique to see how well many of their students truly understand and can explain key concepts. In many cases, the teachers learn something new about the material from the student.

Showing or explaining a concept to you will challenge your child to think and verbalize. Your child will have to review the concept mentally before selecting the best way to explain it to you. This teaching opportunity that you create for your child will further challenge your child's understanding of the material. Your child will also be better prepared for the challenges regarding this concept that will surely come in class and on tests.

Examples of open ended questions where you challenge your child to teach you:

Can you take me through this math problem? It looks quite challenging. **How** did you do it?

How would you teach me to do this problem?

When it comes to science, I never really understood the difference between mammals and reptiles.

What would you say are the main differences?

What are the differences between a senator and someone who serves in the House of Representatives? It looks like they do the same work to me.

Who would you say is more important in our government, a senator or a governor? **Why?**

If you decided to serve in government, **what** position would you choose? **Why?**

Bill of Rights

Open ended:
I have not thought about this in a long time. **Why** do we have a Bill of Rights?

Follow ups:
Remind me again, **what** is an amendment?

In your opinion, **what** are the three most important amendments in the Bill of Rights? **Why?**

If you could add one amendment to the Bill of Rights, **what** would it be?

If you could delete one amendment, **what** would it be?

How does an amendment become law?

As you can see, even if you don't know the material very well, or at all, you can still initiate dialogue that encourages your child to teach you and share their understanding. Some questions are designed to elicit correct answers along with a thorough explanation or rationale for the answer your child gives. Other challenges create the opportunity for opinions which require thinking, and perhaps creativity or problem solving, and verbalization.

Again, look at the work coming home from school. Open ended questions will begin the dialogue process and give you a sense of your child's understanding of the material. Follow up questions and slightly more complex questions such as the ones listed below will solidify and build on the knowledge base.

> **What** is the difference between (this and that)?
>
> If you could add one (delete one), **what** would it be?
>
> **How** would you rank the top three in terms of importance?
>
> **Who/What** is more important?
>
> If you could make one change, **what** would it be?

Whether you challenge your child with open ended and follow up questions, or you challenge your child to teach and explain, your child will understand the key materials in more depth and verbalize their understanding more clearly. Doing so will add to your child's confidence for upcoming classes and tests.

Homework Review

A lot of times, kids do schoolwork without really thinking about the focus of the assignment or the bigger picture. While you can use Challenge Your Child to review homework question by question or answer by answer, this approach might add to your dialogue and your child's depth of understanding:

Open ended:

What is the major focus of this homework assignment?

What did this homework assignment help you learn?

Follow ups:

How well do you feel you understand this concept?

What was the toughest part of the assignment?

Can you give me an example of **where** you would use this concept in daily life?

How does this concept tie into what you have already studied in this class?

How does this concept tie into what you will be studying next?

This approach might improve your child's overall understanding of the material they are learning, and how it fits into the bigger picture of the subject, or even more broadly beyond the subject matter. You have created a unique approach for challenge, dialogue, and increased learning. In the end, these discussions will add to your child's depth of knowledge and understanding.

Examples Outside of School:

There are many challenge possibilities outside of schoolwork that can add to or reinforce your child's knowledge and understanding of key concepts.

 At a Restaurant
Let's say you are having a family meal at a restaurant. When the bill comes, you might ask the following:

Open ended:
We have five people eating dinner. Our bill is 60 dollars. **What** was the average cost per person?

Follow ups:
If I leave 15% for tip for the service, **how** much will I be adding to the cost?

If I leave 20%, **how** much would it be?

Why do we leave tips?

Tax on our meal was 5%, which was included in the 60-dollar amount. Approximately, **what** was the cost for the tax? **How** did you figure this out?

What is sales tax used for?

Travel

Let's say you are driving to visit grandparents for a holiday. The trip is 260 miles. You could ask the following:

Open ended:
Our trip is 260 miles. If we average 65 miles per hour for the trip, **how** long will it take?

Follow ups:
Let's say we average 50 miles an hour due to construction and stops. Approximately **how** much additional time would it take us? **How** did you figure this out?

Gas costs $2.50 per gallon and our car gets 20 miles to the gallon. Approximately **what** will our gas cost for this trip? **How** did you figure this out?

Shopping

Let's say you are shopping with your child for clothes. You come across a $30 item but a sign on the rack says everything is 50% off. You might ask the following:

> **Open ended:**
> **What** will the price be, once adjusted for the 50% discount?
>
> **Follow ups:**
> **What** would the cost be if the discount was 25%?
>
> If I buy three of these items at a 50% discount, **what** would the price be?
>
> There is a 6% sales tax on the items. **What** will be the tax for the three discounted items?
>
> **Why** do stores run sales?
>
> **How** do stores make money if they lower their prices with sales?
>
> If you owned a store, **what** are 2-3 key things you would do to be profitable?

Sports Statistics

Sports statistics can be a great way to create challenges and dialogue about percentages. This can be especially helpful for students who enjoy sports but have less focus on schoolwork. Challenges here can help to show the connection between an activity the child may enjoy and an important math concept.

Let's say you are watching a baseball game on TV with your child. A player comes up to bat and the batting average is displayed on the screen. It shows that the player has a batting average of 300 for the season. You might ask the following:

Open ended:
It looks like this player has a .300 batting average. **How** was this determined?

If your child knows the answer and understands the process, you can compliment and follow up. If your child does not know, you can explain how this percentage is figured out and create a follow up question to check for understanding.

Possible follow up questions depending on your child's understanding of this concept:
If a player had 2 at bats and 1 hit, **what** would the batting average be?

If a player had 10 at bats and 4 hits, **what** would the batting average be?

If a player had 100 at bats and 27 hits, **what** would the batting average be?

Why are batting averages important?

How are percentages or averages used in other sports to determine a player's or a team's success?

Can *Challenge Your Child* be used with high school students and beyond? Absolutely! This questioning method is a teaching concept used in medical school, law school, and graduate programs. Corporations sometimes use this approach in their training programs with case studies.

In higher levels of education, it is often up to the student to take greater responsibility for their learning. Students are expected to teach themselves and prepare for classroom challenges, exams and projects as best as possible. It is up to the teacher to assess what the students know and what they need to learn. They do so by challenging. Sometimes a teacher may ask four or five questions in dialogue with one student in class to test their depth of knowledge. If a student does not know an answer, the teacher can quickly move on to another student who may be able to answer correctly. Excellence, or lack of understanding or preparation, is on display in these settings. If needed, the teacher can fill in the gaps of knowledge, creating key teaching and learning moments.

Kids are often bored with lectures, or by being taught something they already know. Kids are never bored when they are challenged. Challenging as a teaching tool sparks dialogue, debate, and increased understanding. Students taught with the challenge method study harder in order to be more prepared for the challenging questions to come, and in order to succeed with the inevitable competition from other students.

A teacher quickly assesses what students know and don't know. The teacher also identifies who is the most knowledgeable, who is the least, and if the student can apply their knowledge in a variety of ways. Students taught with the challenge method are always thinking, "What else might be asked, or what else will I need to know?" They have to anticipate. The anticipation mindset will serve your child well moving forward in their education and career.

Let's look at some examples with high school-age children. As mentioned with younger students, the homework review can be a very helpful approach. Setting up challenges where your child teaches you can also be very helpful in creating dialogue and giving your child the opportunity to verbalize their understanding of any key concepts you choose to discuss.

If your child is taking literature classes, they will read and discuss in class many different books or stories. You might be able to read some of the same material they are studying and have discussions with your child about the text. Your open ended questions and follow up questions will challenge your child's understanding of the material, depth of knowledge of the material, and the ability to share thoughts and opinions about key points from the readings. This dialogue can help your child to be well prepared for the classroom discussions and tests that will come.

Examples Pertaining to School:

Math and science concepts at the high school level can be very challenging. Again, these classes and the material being studied offer great opportunities for you to ask your child to teach you.

 You can pick a particular math problem and ask:

Open ended:
How did you go about solving this problem?

Follow ups:
Pick another problem. Ask: **How** would you teach me to do this problem?

Follow up by picking a similar problem and see if you can do it, and then complete the problem. Ask: **How** did I do here?

Foreign Languages

Foreign language study creates a great opportunity to let your child teach you. Mastering a language requires constant thinking and verbalization. With particular words or phrases, you can ask:

How would you teach me to say this word or phrase? (in the language being studied)

What did you learn in (language) class today? **What** examples can you share or teach me?

You can pick a paragraph from a newspaper or book and ask your child, **how** would you translate this passage in the language you are studying?

You might pick a passage from your child's foreign language textbook and ask, **how** would you describe what this passage says?

You might also pick a particular issue or topic and ask your child, **how** would you write a story or an opinion about this topic in the language you are studying?

You might ask, if you become proficient in this language, **what** particular job opportunities might be available to you after graduation? **What** opportunity do you think you might enjoy the most?

Social studies and current events offer great opportunities to challenge thinking, problem solving, and verbalization. Whether it is world history, American history, civics or current events, there are many topics to understand and discuss.

History

Let's say your child is studying World War II as part of American history. You might ask the following:

Open ended:

What were the key events that led to America becoming involved in World War II?

Follow ups:

How were the events that led to World War II different than events leading to World War I?

What are some of the key events in World War II that are most concerning or important to you?

Who are individuals from World War II who most impressed you and **why**?

In your opinion, **what** could have been done to prevent World War II?

When discussing history, comparisons are a great way to challenge thinking.

> **How** would you compare two presidents?
>
> **How** would living in Russia be different than living in the United States?
>
> **How** are capitalism and socialism alike? **How** are they different?

Several follow up questions can add to the depth of the discussion.

 Current Events

Regarding current events, let's say you read an important news story online. You ask your child to read the story as well to increase their awareness of the situation. After, you might ask:

> Open ended:
> **What** are your thoughts on this issue (or the person) involved?

> Follow ups:
> **What** impact do you think this event will have going forward?
>
> **What** concerns you most about what you read here?
>
> If you were involved in this issue, **how** would you have reacted? **What** would you have done?

Test Preparation

Often times parents will ask children if they are prepared for an upcoming test. Students can be vague in their responses. Many parents can be uncertain how to help.

Let's say your child has an important science test coming up. To open the conversation you might ask:

Open ended:

How challenging will your Science test be tomorrow?

Follow ups:

What will the test format be?

How will the test format impact the way you study?

What will 2-3 of the main focus points be for the test?

How would you explain your understanding of this material?

What potential surprise questions from class discussions might be on the test?

If you were the teacher, **what** two or three questions would you definitely ask if you were creating the test?

Examples Outside of School:

Your high school-aged child will soon be on their own to a greater degree. Whether getting ready to work a part-time job during school to help with college expenses or getting ready for work life after school, there are many issues and challenges to be faced in adult work life. Your child will need a wide variety of life knowledge to help with key decisions.

Budgeting

Let's say your child is getting ready to go back to school and you create a budget for clothes and accessories based on what you can afford, or think is reasonable. You tell your child you have $200 to buy clothes and accessories for the start of the school year.

Open ended:

How can you get the most purchasing power out of this budget?

Follow ups:

What are the most important items you need to buy?

What items will you have to pass up or buy at a later time?

If there is something you really want but the cost is beyond your budget, **how** will you plan to ultimately make the purchase?

Why is it important to budget your money and keep track of expenses?

What are some of the major expenses we as parents have to budget for each month and annually?

Auto Insurance
Let's say your child just received their driver's license. You could share a copy of the previous car insurance bill and the new bill with your child's cost added in. This can create many discussion points.

Open ended:
Here is our car insurance bill for the next 6 months. Here is a breakdown of the costs with you added in.

Why do you need to be covered with auto insurance?

Follow ups:
What is the difference between collision insurance and liability insurance?

What is a deductible? **What** are your thoughts on deductibles?

What are the best actions you can take to prevent having a car accident?

If you are in an accident and you are not injured, **what** actions should you take?

What actions can you take to lower auto insurance rates?

What other types of insurance do you think you will need as you get older? **Why**?

TAX Taxes/Deductions

Children (teenagers) are sometimes surprised when they receive their first paycheck. It will be their first introduction to taxes and deductions, something that will be in place for the entirety of their work life. They know the hours they worked, and the pay rate they had agreed upon. That said, when they see their check and pay stub, they may be shocked if they do not understand deductions and why they exist. This creates a great opportunity for discussion.

Open ended:

What were your thoughts on your first paycheck? **What** were you expecting to receive?

Follow ups:

What was the total percentage of money earned that you kept, after taxes and deductions?

What are the deductions you see listed? **What** is each deduction for?

What do you know about Social Security? **How** does Social Security work?

What are your thoughts about having taxes deducted from your earnings?

Why is it important to check or double check the calculations and deductions on your paystub?

As you begin full-time work, **what** other deductions or withholdings will potentially come from your pay?

Beyond High School

As your child enters college or the work world, they will be on their own to a greater degree. You will not be present to challenge. That said, the process you have used with them over the years can now serve as a study guide, a test prep guide, or a judgment and assessment process in the workplace. The difference is, instead of being challenged by you, the child can now use this process to guide their own study, thinking, and planning. The ability to anticipate challenges and needs will be play a key role in your child's success as they move on in higher education and the work world.

Examples Pertaining to School:

Test Preparation:
Imagine your child studying for a college exam with the following thought process:

Open ended:
What are the major concepts that I will absolutely need to know for this exam?

Follow ups:
What will the test format be and how should this impact the way I prepare?

How well do I really know this material?

What will be the toughest material for me on this exam?

What material do I need to study more thoroughly in order to perform well?

What other potential key points covered in class lecture or discussion will be on the test?

Where might I be challenged to go into greater depth with my knowledge?

Study Group

Let's say your child is part of a study group that works together in preparing for key projects or exams. The challenge process can be used to create discussion and debate to help ensure the entire group performs well.

Open ended:

What are the key points ranked 1-5 that we absolutely need to know to score well on this exam or project?

The debate and discussion here not only create a priority list; through the dialogue, the students begin to enhance their learning.

Follow ups:

What will the test format or project requirements be and how should we prepare?

Who has the best insight into each priority and how can we use this understanding to help the rest of the group perform well?

Where might we possibly be challenged to go into greater depth with our knowledge and understanding of the material?

If working on a project, **what** else can we do to stand out with the presentation and/or results for this project?

Who else should we talk to for insight on how to be prepared for the best possible results?

What are we missing in our preparation?

Examples Outside of School:

A Work Project

Imagine your child working a job after high school, or perhaps taking an intern role during summers while in college. The boss has given your child a project to be completed. This could be a key opportunity!

Open ended:
What exactly will I need to do to create success with this project?

Follow ups:
What will be my top three priorities with this project?

Who can I talk with, or who could mentor me, to help me better understand what is needed for success?

What materials, funding, or further information will I need to create success with this project?

What am I missing?

How will I ultimately present my results to the boss and **how** should I prepare?

How will my work or findings make things better for my boss and the organization?

How is this project potentially connected to other work going on in the organization?

These are just a few examples of how *Challenge Your Child* concepts can be used as your child moves forward in creating their own success in higher education and the workplace.

Imagine your child in college level pre-med or pre-law classes where competitive performance, test scores, and references dictate the future options in these careers.

Envision your child as a recent college graduate interviewing for a lucrative position that opens the doors to incredible opportunity.

Think about your child working in an engineering or architectural firm. The company is struggling to solve a challenging problem and your child has a potential solution to present that might be in the best interest of the organization.

Imagine your child as a salesperson in a key selling situation. A major contract is on the line and the interaction between your child and the customer will determine if and when the deal moves forward, potentially bringing success for all involved.

See your child sitting in a corporate boardroom participating in key decision-making discussions that will determine the company's success moving forward.

Imagine your child planning to start a new business and trying to figure out all the ways to create success, and how to gain the financing to start up.

These are just a few of the many possible situations, challenges, and opportunities that young people could face—and excel with—as their lives and careers move forward. This does not even take into account all the important life decisions ahead.

In the end, your child's confidence in their ability to think, problem solve, and verbalize will go a long way in helping them anticipate, prepare, and achieve. Your involvement now, each and every day, will help your child to be better prepared for the competitive challenges and key decisions to come.

Challenge Your Child will help you play a greater role in helping your child prepare for academic excellence and success in life. I hope that the examples I shared for various age levels show how open ended questions, follow up questions, and repetition can create the dialogue necessary to challenge your child to think, problem solve, and verbalize. With your consistent effort, you can have an amazing impact in helping your child learn and succeed.

This should be fun! Focus on a few interactions each day. Be positive!

Be patient with yourself and your child. If you and your child have never done anything like this before, it may take a while for both of you to get into the habit and enjoy.

Don't worry about mistakes or possibly a day where your child is not willing to engage. Try again the day after. As long as you don't quit, you and your child will gain.

Be prepared to get more involved in your child's education.

Be prepared to help take your child's education to the next level.

Challenge Your Child!

At this point, you may still have a few questions about moving forward with Challenge Your Child. Below are questions that other readers have asked me, and I hope my answers may help as you begin.

How do I go about creating the questions? Where do I find the time?

Once you understand the Challenge Your Child process, the questions will come to you easily. In fact, every time you look at a book, read an article, or have a discussion, you will see the opportunity for open ended questions and dialogue. You will be amazed at the educational interactions you can have with your child and how much you can contribute to your child's learning.

How will I know if my questions are age appropriate?

If your questions are too easy, your child will answer quickly and confidently. Give your child positive feedback for the good answer and try something a little more challenging. This is what teachers do. Great teachers learn the capability of each student and find ways to challenge each at their own level. Open ended questions will bring you to the threshold of what your child knows or needs to learn. Follow up questions will help you take learning and understanding to the next level.

What if my question is too difficult?

You never know what a child might know. You also never know what a child might be able to figure out on their own. If your challenge is too hard, your child will answer "I don't know" and you can scale it back. You will also have a teaching moment as you explain the importance or significance of the answer to the question you asked. You can follow up by asking the question again to see if your child understands. Whether your child figures out an answer, or you help with an explanation, teaching and learning occur.

I am not a teacher. I don't know what to teach or how to teach. Should I do this?

You don't need to be a teacher. Rather, focus on the opportunities you have every day to challenge your child to think, problem solve, and verbalize. Can you think of more important skills? Throughout this book, I have presented several examples in a variety of situations to help you contribute to your child's learning, even if it's a subject area where you have little to no expertise.

CPSIA information can be obtained
at www.ICGtesting.com
Printed in the USA
LVHW050917250122
709251LV00010B/270

9 798764 722580